U.S. Fish & Wildlife Service

National Fish Passage Program

Reconnecting Aquatic Species to Historical Habitats

Program Accomplishments 1999-2001

Foreword

The Nation's fisheries, and the economies they support, depend on the ability of fish to gain access to healthy aquatic habitats. Fish in lakes, rivers, and estuaries need to migrate to vital habitats for spawning, feeding, and growth. Yet millions of artificial barriers block fish movements in the United States. To address this problem, the Service's Fisheries Program established the National Fish Passage Program in 1999. This report tells what we have done since the Program's inception to provide new paths to old homes for America's fish populations.

The Fish Passage Program is an outstanding example of a voluntary, habitat-based approach to fisheries conservation. The program is citizen centered and produces impressive on-the-ground results, restoring unimpeded flows and fish migration in partnership with Federal, State, Tribal and local governments, non-governmental organizations, and private landowners.

Loss and alteration of aquatic habitats are principal factors in the decline of native fish and other aquatic resources. Obsolete dams, poorly designed culverts, and unscreened water diversions degrade aquatic habitat throughout the nation. With recent improvements in water quality, and effective harvest management practices in place, restoring fish passage is one of the most far-reaching measures we can take to conserve fishery resources. The Service looks forward to continuing and expanding its alliance with our partners on this important initiative.

Steve Williams

Director
U.S. Fish and Wildlife Service

Table of Contents

Introduction

Early in our history, rivers ran wild, and fish followed them according to their needs. In the ensuing years, America fueled the Industrial Revolution with resources of water, timber, minerals and wildlife. Early American innovation and progress were generally oblivious to their dependence on the fragile natural world. American resources seemed abundant without end. Then the fish began to disappear.

All river fish migrate between feeding and spawning areas and make other seasonal movements to important habitats. Barriers prevent natural fish migrations, keeping them from these habitats. As a result, some populations of native fish are gone and others are in drastic decline.

Millions of culverts, dikes, water diversions, dams, and other artificial barriers were constructed to impound and redirect water for irrigation, flood control, electricity, drinking water, and transportation— all changing natural features of rivers and streams. After more than three centuries of building dams and other barriers on rivers and streams, many Americans are increasingly concerned about their effects on fish and other aquatic species. Many dams are obsolete and no longer serve their original purpose. Culverts that funnel water beneath roads and train tracks often pose insurmountable barriers to fish.

In 1999, the U.S. Fish and Wildlife Service initiated the National Fish Passage Program to work with others to address these problems. The purposes of this report are to describe the Program, its activities and accomplishments from 1999 through 2001, and the role and contributions of partners and stakeholders in accomplishing these results.

National Fish Passage Program

Through its National Fish Passage Program, the U.S. Fish and Wildlife Service uses a voluntary, non-regulatory approach to remove and bypass barriers. The Program addresses the problem of fish barriers on a national level, working with local communities and partner agencies to restore natural flows and fish migration. The Program is administered by National and Regional Coordinators and delivered by Fish and Wildlife Management Assistance Offices, with 300 biologists located across the Nation. Appropriations for the Program support the Coordinators, in-the-water fish passage projects, and the Fish Passage Decision Support System (described below). The Program provides technical assistance and funding to assist others in restoring fish passage. Types of assistance include providing information on fish and habitat needs and methods for fish to bypass barriers.

Fish Passage Decision Support System

The Fish Passage Decision Support System assists the Service and its partners in planning and prioritizing fish passage projects. The system is a geographically-referenced database of barriers preventing fish movement, including barrier location, type, size, owner and passage capabilities, associated fish species, and habitat information. By early 2003, the system will provide an on-line data entry and mapping utility program, with analytical Geographic Information System (GIS) capabilities. The user will be able to 'point-and-click' on existing barriers for displaying information at that location and point to rivers and streams to identify new barrier locations for data entry. Analytical capabilities will include the capacity to calculate river miles opened after barrier removal. Integration with GIS software increases the capabilities of fisheries scientists to make better management decisions, prioritize fish passage projects, identify critical areas, and implement projects.

Currently, the database incorporates information from the Army Corps of Engineers' National Inventory of Dams, state dam databases from North Carolina and Tennessee, and a regional database (StreamNet) from the Pacific States Marine Fisheries Commission. Service biologists will be entering additional data from inventory projects. Smaller dams, culverts, dikes, and irrigation diversions will be added from national, state, and local sources. Also, a partnership is in place for developing and incorporating a stream module of the Multi-State Aquatic Resources Information System (MARIS), which will compile State stream fisheries databases.

Program Goal

To restore native fish and other aquatic species to self-sustaining levels by reconnecting habitat that has been fragmented by barriers, where such re-connection would not result in a net negative ecological effect such as providing increased habitat to exotic species.

Fish Passage Program Funding History

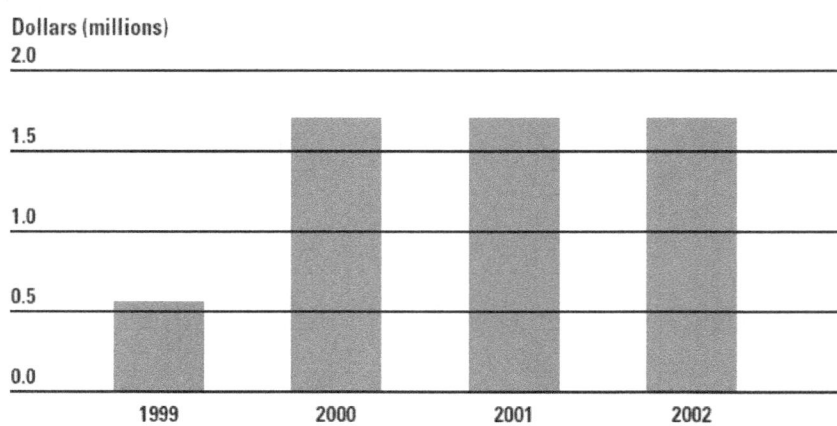

Dollars (millions)

Program Accomplishments

Since 1999, the Fish Passage Program has:

- Supported 76 fish passage projects with over 141 different partners,

- Restored access to over 3,443 miles of river habitat and 65,088 acres of wetlands for fish spawning and growth, and

- Leveraged partner contributions totaling $6.2 million, compared to the Program investment of $2.3 million.

Restoring fish passage benefits people, fish and other animals. Fish passage projects increase habitat available for fish spawning and growth. Anglers, and commercial and subsistence fishers benefit from larger fish populations, which are distributed across more available habitats. Natural flows and temperature are restored for salmon, trout, sturgeon, striped bass, herring and shad, paddlefish, and many more native and declining forage and game species. Fish-eating birds such as eagles, ospreys and kingfishers have more forage, and bears, otters and mink benefit from larger fish populations.

Eighteen endangered, threatened, or candidate aquatic species populations have directly benefitted from fish passage projects, including:

- Atlantic Salmon
- Chinook Salmon
- Coho Salmon
- Chum Salmon
- Steelhead
- Arctic Grayling
- Apache Trout
- Lahontan Cuttroat Trout
- Bull Trout
- Pallid Sturgeon
- Shortnose Sturgeon
- Gila Chub
- Leopard Darter
- Loach Minnow
- Cui-ui
- Topeka Shiner
- Cape Fear Shiner
- Plain Pocketbook Mussel

Emptying fish trap to evaluate fish passage effectiveness at Mattamuskeet NWR, NC.

Financial Investment in Project Completion

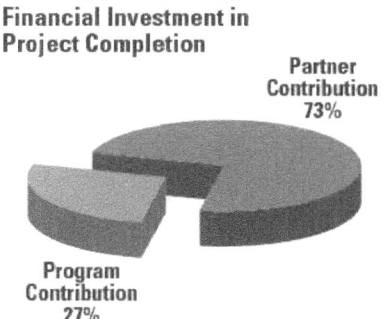

Partner Contribution 73%

Program Contribution 27%

The following pages identify, by Region, all projects initiated or completed through 2001 and highlights 27 projects with a brief description. For more information on the projects, visit the Program web site at http://fisheries.fws.gov/fwsma/fishpassage.

Culvert renovation on Duck Creek, AK.

Dam removal on Conodoguinet Creek, PA.

Region 1 – Pacific

Douglas DeHart – Fish Passage
Program Coordinator
U.S. Fish and Wildlife Service
911 N.E. 11th Avenue
Portland, OR 97232-4181

Fish passage has been and continues to be a major issue in fishery resource protection, restoration, and enhancement in the Pacific Region. Water diversions and associated dams redirect and impound water from streams and rivers for crop irrigation, flood control, hydroelectric power, drinking water, and other beneficial purposes. Many farms and ranches in the West are irrigated by water diverted from rivers and streams into irrigation canals. Water diversions can block normal migration of fish, and diversion of fish into pumps, pipes, irrigation canals, and fields can greatly reduce their survival.

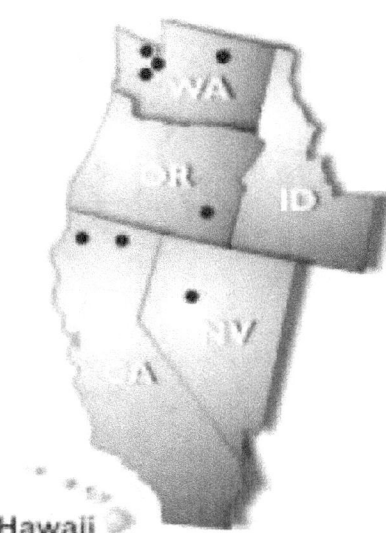

Location of Fish Passage Program projects in Region 1, 1999-2001

National Fish Passage Program projects in USFWS Region 1, 1999-2001

State	Project Title	Project Type	Year Funded
WA	Tahuya River (Buffin Creek)*	Culvert Renovation	1999
WA	Tahuya River (WRIA 15-0470)*	Culvert Renovation	1999
WA	Icicle Creek	Fishway Design	1999
CA	Mynot Creek	Culvert Renovation	2000
OR	Blitzen River, Malheur NWR*	Fish Screens	2000
NV	Truckee River	Fish Screen Renovation	2001
WA	Skobob Creek	Culvert Renovation	2001
CA	Little Shasta River*	Dam Removal and Screening	2001

* Highlighted on the following pages.

Since 1999, the Fish Passage Program has implemented 8 fish passage projects, including culvert renovations, fishways, dam removals, and fish screening structures. These projects have provided uninhibited access to over 123 miles of river and stream habitat, and 1,100 acres of wetland habitat, for fish spawning, rearing and growth.

In 2002, new cost-share funding opportunities became available through the U.S. Fish and Wildlife Service for voluntary fish screening and passage projects associated with water diversions in Idaho, Oregon, and Washington. Fish screens placed at entrances to water diversions can prevent juvenile salmon from swimming into irrigation canals, thereby decreasing mortality for these and other native fishes.

These partners contributed funds and cooperative efforts toward accomplishments in restoring fish passage in Region 1. Their contributions are gratefully acknowledged.

- U.S. Bureau of Reclamation
- U.S. Forest Service
- U.S. Environmental Protection Agency
- National Fish and Wildlife Foundation
- Yakama Nation, WA
- Pyramid Lake Paiute Tribe, NV
- Yurok Tribe, CA
- Oregon Department of Fish and Wildlife
- Washington Department of Natural Resources Jobs for the Environment
- Del Norte County, CA
- Mason County Department of Public Works, WA
- California Conservation Corp
- Reid Realty, WA
- Hood Canal Enhancement Group, WA
- Volunteer Services, WA
- Washington Aquatic Land Enhancement Action
- Ducks Unlimited

Tahuya River, Washington

2 Projects

Project Description:

Buffin Creek and unnamed stream WRIA 15-0470 are tributaries to the Tahuya River, which is located on the Kitsap Peninsula in western Washington. The Tahuya River discharges into the Hood Canal fjord of Puget Sound. The upper reaches of these streams had been inaccessible to anadromous salmonids due to blockage by poorly sized and placed road culverts.

Culvert on Buffin Creek before renovation.

Culvert on Buffin Creek after renovation.

Project Method:

The former undersized culvert on Buffin Creek was replaced with a pipe arch culvert. The culvert was laid flat and countersunk, and three log weirs were installed to adjust the stream grade. Gravel was placed to restore the stream bed, and rock riprap was placed to maintain road bank stability. On the unnamed stream, the culvert remained; however, five log weirs were installed to provide step pools with adequate water depths for fish passage.

Project Outcomes (Benefits):

Renovation of both culverts opened up 4.5 miles of stream habitat within 2,210 acres of relatively undisturbed watershed area. In addition, 113 acres of wetland habitat are associated with these stream segments. Correcting these passage barriers provided unrestricted access to former spawning and rearing habitats for adult and juvenile coho salmon, steelhead trout, and cutthroat trout. Replacement of the Buffin Creek culvert also allows for more natural transport of woody debris and sediment through the system.

Partners:

Reid Realty, Hood Canal Enhancement Group, Volunteer Services, Washington Aquatic Land Enhancement Action, Mason County Department of Public Works, Washington Department of Natural Resources Jobs for the Environment, and private landowners.

For more information contact:

Western Washington Fishery Resources Office, 2625 Parkmont Lane, Building A, Olympia, WA 98502

Culvert on unnamed stream before renovation

Step pools installed after renovation

Project Funding

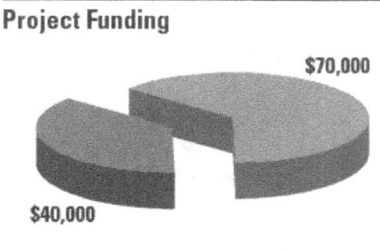

$70,000

$40,000

▨ FWS Fish Passage   ▨ Partners

Blitzen River, Malheur NWR, Oregon

Project Description:

Historically, Mud Creek and Bridge Creek were direct tributaries to the Blitzen River. Today, these systems are altered and water is mixed due to diversion dams and canals. Blitzen River is re-directed into the West Canal and the East Canal, with Mud Creek and Bridge Creek flowing into the East Canal. A portion of the mixed water is then returned to Bridge Creek, and eventually to the Blitzen River. Historically, limited fish passage was provided. Malheur National Wildlife Refuge has committed to providing fish passage throughout this system for redband trout to reconnect them to historical habitats and natural movements. Several fish screening devices and fishways have been installed; however, several passage and screening problems remain unresolved.

Project Methods:

At the Bridge Creek headgates, four inverted weirs are being constructed below the headgates to dissipate the undershot flows. Immediately below the gaging station weir, a small log and rock weir is being constructed to create a jump pool. At the Blitzen River headgates, one of the three existing headgates have been removed and a Denil fishway is being installed in its place.

Other fish screen projects, some with fish ladders, have been completed on the Refuge. These prevent fish entrainment and diversion into pipes and canals.

Headgate at the Bridge Creek/East Canal Bridge creates a barrier at high flows

Bridge Creek gaging station creates passage barrier during low flows

Downstream view of the headgate at East Canal/Blitzen River

Upstream view of the headgate at East Canal/Blitzen River

Project Outcomes (Benefits):
When all fish passage projects are complete, approximately six miles of important spawning habitat in Bridge and Mud creeks will be reconnected with the Blitzen River and Malheur Lake. The refuge will provide further protection to redband trout and secure eight miles of habitat in the lower Blitzen River drainage by providing passage in East Canal. The Refuge will also reconnect East Canal, Boca Lake, Bridge Creek and Mud Creek with over 65 miles of the upper Blitzen River and tributaries. The projects in East Canal and Bridge Creek will directly benefit redband trout, mountain whitefish and other native fish species in the Blitzen River watershed.

Partners:
Oregon Department of Fish and Wildlife, National Fish and Wildlife Foundation, and Ducks Unlimited.

For more information contact:
U.S. Fish and Wildlife Service, Malheur National Wildlife Refuge, HC 72 Box 245, Princeton, OR 97721

Solar-powered fish screen on Bridge Creek

Rotary drum fish screen on East Canal

Fish screen with ladder on East Canal

Project Funding

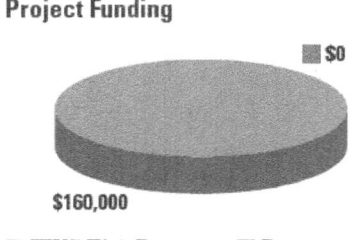

$0

$160,000

■ FWS Fish Passage ■ Partners

Region 2 – Southwest

Bob Pitman – Fish Passage
Program Coordinator
U.S. Fish and Wildlife Service
P.O. Box 1306, Room 3118
Albuquerque, NM 87103-1306

The Fisheries Program in the Southwest Region focuses on interjurisdictional fishery resources, fishery resources on Indian Reservations or National Wildlife Refuges, fisheries lost to federal water development projects, recovery of species protected under the *Endangered Species Act*, restoring depleted fish populations, and non-indigenous aquatic nuisance species.

Between 1999 and 2001, the Southwest Region has implemented seven fish passage projects, including culvert renovations, repairing low flow road crossings, and restructuring water control structures. Over 51 miles of stream habitat has been opened up for spawning, rearing and feeding to benefit Apache trout, leopard darter, Ouachita shiner, Gila chub, desert sucker, and other native species.

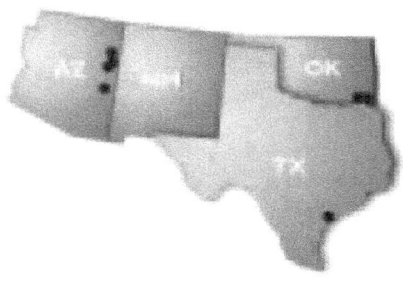

Location of Fish Passage Program projects in Region 2, 1999-2001

National Fish Passage Program projects in USFWS Region 2, 1999-2001

State	Project Title	Project Type	Year Funded
AZ	Blue River Road Crossing*	Low-flow Road Crossing	2000
AZ	Geronimo's Cave*	Flow Improvement	2000
OK	Little River at Horseshoe Bend	Low-flow Road Crossing	2000
AZ	Firebox Creek	Culvert Renovation	2001
AZ	Pacheta Creek	Culvert Renovation	2001
OK	Honobia Creek at Bridge Three*	Culvert/Road Restoration	2001
TX	Foester Lake, Aransas NWR	Water Control Structure	2001

* Highlighted on the following pages.

These partners contributed funds and cooperative efforts toward accomplishments in restoring fish passage in Region 2. Their contributions are gratefully acknowledged.

- U.S. Bureau of Indian Affairs
- San Carlos Apache Tribal Roads Department, AZ
- San Carlos Apache Tribal Recreation and Wildlife Department, AZ
- White Mountain Apache Tribe, AZ
- Oklahoma Department of Wildlife Conservation
- Texas Department of Parks and Wildlife
- Kansas Department of Wildlife and Parks
- John Hancock Timber Industries, OK
- Ash Creek Cattle Association, AZ
- Aluminum Company of America, TX

Blue River Road Crossing, Arizona

Project Description:

The Blue River is located on the San Carlos Apache Indian Reservation, in the east-central portion of Arizona. The objective of the Blue River Fish Passage Project was to armor the wet road crossing at the junction of the 1200 Road and the Blue River.

Stream bed disturbance from vehicle and road maintenance equipment was creating erosion and water quality issues in the Blue River. The San Carlos Tribal Roads Department had traditionally addressed these issues by installing culverts; however, this project was designed to demonstrate an alternative to culverts that also did not create a fish passage barrier.

Project Method:

Cooperators installed a series of precast cement slabs with galvanized steel cables used to link them together to form a mat on the stream bed. The precast slabs were installed by hand, minimizing the need for heavy equipment, thereby reducing the disturbance to the stream bed. Spacing between the slabs allows for the movement of fish even during periods of low flow. Following the construction of the mat, cement slabs were poured on the banks adjacent to the mat, which were designed to stabilize the stream banks and add an additional anchor for the structure.

Project Outcomes (Benefits):

The Blue River contains a secure native fish assemblage that includes the Gila chub, a candidate for listing under the Endangered Species Act. Vehicle movement across Blue River has been enhanced by minimizing the erosion and water quality problems experienced before the project. Fish have been observed passing through the structure, both during and after the project.

Road traffic over Blue River

Hand-placing precast slabs

Completed road crossing restoration project

Partners:

San Carlos Recreation and Wildlife Department, U.S. Bureau of Indian Affairs Land Operations, San Carlos Apache Tribal Roads Department, and the Ash Creek Cattle Association.

For more information contact:

Arizona Fishery Resources Office – San Carlos, P.O. Box 710, Peridot, AZ 85542

Project Funding

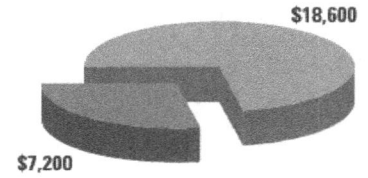

$18,600

$7,200

■ FWS Fish Passage ■ Partners

Geronimo's Cave Irrigation Diversion, Arizona

Project Description:
The East Fork of the White River, a tributary of the Salt River, is located on the Fort Apache Indian Reservation, home of the White Mountain Apache Tribe. The Tribe currently manages the river for the protection of sensitive, federally threatened, and native species, as well as an Apache trout recreational fishery. The Tribe also depends upon the river to provide water for agriculture. Throughout the lower reaches of the river there are numerous irrigation diversions. Routine annual repair and

Inadequate conditions at Geronimo's Cave irrigation diversion, preventing fish passage

Eroding banks at Geronimo's Cave irrigation diversion

maintenance of these diversions is conducted; however, there was concern that some diversions were preventing upstream movement of fish during high flows with high sediment transport.

Project Method:
Cooperators designed a modified version of a cross vane weir. In addition to the weir, native plants were transplanted to prevent bank erosion. The cross vane weir shape was selected for the purpose of directing water flow through the irrigation ditch, but also away from the stream banks. The new design provides for delivery of water to the irrigation ditch and re-directs water flow to the center of the stream channel, and away from eroded banks.

Project Outcomes (Benefits):
Preliminary findings from seasonal evaluations suggest that the redesign of Geronimo's Cave diversion has maintained natural channel morphology. Particular signs of improvement include: less dramatic change in channel gradient, no braiding upstream of the channel, no scour pool below the diversion, and no bank erosion occurring around the diversion. Species benefitted by the project include the threatened Apache trout and loach minnow; desert sucker; Sonora sucker; and speckled dace.

The new design of the Geronimo's Cave irrigation diversion

Partners:
White Mountain Apache Tribe Watershed Program, Hydrology Department, Wildlife and Outdoor Recreation Division, and Land Operations Division.

For more information contact:
Arizona Fishery Resources Office – Pinetop, P.O. Box 39, Pinetop, AZ 85935

Honobia Creek at Bridge Three, Oklahoma

Project Description:
The Little River Fish Passage Project was a cooperative effort with private landowners that restored the natural function of this river, where fish and other aquatic species could utilize all stream segments and still allow responsible harvest of timber in the area. Honobia Creek is a tributary to the Little River. This low water crossing presented an impediment to fish passage because the arch pipes funnel a large volume of water through a narrow culvert creating abnormally high water velocities within the culvert. At high flows, the stream cuts the stream bed downstream of the structure creating a waterfall, which made it particularly difficult for fish passage at low water.

Project Method:
The project replaced the embedded culvert type crossing with a box culvert structure. Vehicular traffic continues at this site.

Project Outcomes (Benefits):
This project facilitates the genetic exchange between fragmented populations of Ouachita shiner (species of concern) and leopard darter (federally and state threatened) by reconnecting 12 miles of aquatic habitat. It also enhances recreational fishing opportunities for smallmouth bass and spotted bass.

Honobia Creek at Bridge Three before renovation

Honobia Creek at Bridge Three after renovation

Partners:
Oklahoma Department of Wildlife Conservation, Texas Department of Parks and Wildlife, and John Hancock Timber Industries.

For more information contact:
Oklahoma Fishery Resources Office, 5700 West Highway 7, Tishomingo, OK 73460

Project Funding

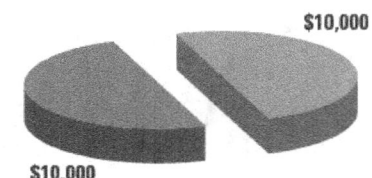

$10,000

$10,000

■ FWS Fish Passage   ■ Partners

Region 3 – Great Lakes-Big Rivers

Mike Hoff – Fish Passage
Program Coordinator
U.S. Fish and Wildlife Service
Federal Building
1 Federal Drive
Fort Snelling, MN 55111

The Great Lakes-Big Rivers Region of the U.S. Fish and Wildlife Service is home to more than thirty million people. The Great Lakes–deep freshwater seas–are the largest system of surface freshwater on the Earth, accounting for more than 90% of the surface freshwater in the U.S. The lakes themselves create unique conditions that support a wealth of biological diversity, including more than 130 rare species and ecosystems. An estimated 180 species of fish are native to the Great Lakes.

The 'Big Rivers' refer to the Mississippi, Missouri, and Ohio Rivers Ecosystem. A total of 157 fish species have been collected in the Upper Mississippi River (UMR), with more than 90% of these classified as native. The Big Rivers support a valuable recreational and commercial fishery. From 1980 to 1995, landings of commercial fish species in the UMR averaged about 10 million pounds with a wholesale value of about $2 million. Common carp, catfish species, buffalo species, carpsucker species, paddlefish, and freshwater drum compose the bulk of this catch.

It has long been recognized that the Great Lakes-Big Rivers' fisheries, and the economies they support, depend on the ability of fish to reach healthy aquatic habitats. Since 1999, Region 3 has initiated 15 fish passage projects through the National Fish Passage Program, including culvert or road crossing renovations, dam removals, and the installation of fish passage structures. These projects have provided access to 162 miles of river habitat and 960 acres of wetland habitat for fish spawning, rearing, and feeding.

National Fish Passage Program projects in USFWS Region 3, 1999-2001

State	Project Title	Project Type	Year Funded
WI	Chippewa River Paddlefish Study	Assessment	1999
MI	Tin Shanty Bridge – Black River*	Culvert Renovation	1999
OH	Western Lake Erie Coastal Wetlands	Fish Passage at Dike	1999-2000
MI	Hardwood Creek	Culvert Renovation	2000
WI	Hornby Creek	Beaver Dam Removal	2000
IA	Western Iowa Streams*	Road Crossing Stabilization	2001
MI	North Branch of Manistee River*	Culvert Renovation	2001
MI	Black River Watershed Inventory	Barrier Inventory	2001
MN	Grand Portage Creek	Culvert Renovation	2001
MN	Little Lake Creek	Culvert Renovation	2001
WI	Graveyard Creek*	Beaver Dam Removal	2001
WI/MI	Building Fish Friendly Stream Crossings	Workshop	2001
MN	Pelican River Dutton Locks*	Dam Removal	2001
MI	McMasters Creek	Culvert Renovation	2001
MI	Stony Creek	Culvert Renovation	2001

* Highlighted on the following pages.

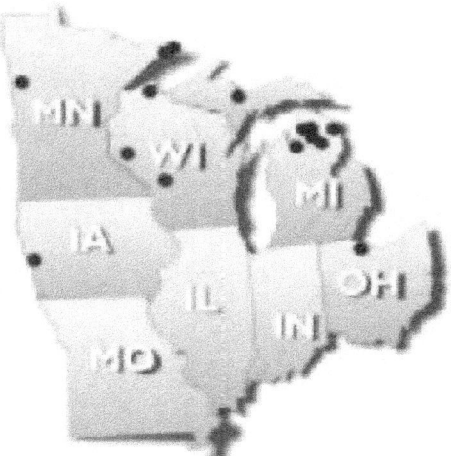

Location of Fish Passage Program projects in Region 3, 1999-2001

Educational workshops have been conducted to promote better fish passage at road crossings. The Ashland Fishery Resources Office sponsored a workshop in 2001 and 2002, entitled, *How to Build Fish Friendly Stream Crossings*. The 2001 workshop, hosted by the Marquette Biological Station, was attended by 20 natural resource managers and landowners.

These partners contributed funds and cooperative efforts toward accomplishments in restoring fish passage in Region 3. Also in 2001, Region 3 was successful in securing $233,000 from the National Fish and Wildlife Foundation (NFWF) to fund fish passage projects in the Region. All contributions are gratefully acknowledged.

- USDA Natural Resources Conservation Service
- U.S. Geological Survey
- National Parks Service
- U.S. Army Corps of Engineers
- USFWS-Partners for Fish and Wildlife Program
- National Fish and Wildlife Foundation
- Bad River Tribe, WI
- Grande Portage Indian Reservation, WI
- Michigan Department of Natural Resources
- Michigan Dept. of Environmental Quality
- Minnesota Department of Natural Resources
- Minnesota Department of Transportation
- Ohio Department of Natural Resources
- Wisconsin Department of Natural Resources
- Kalkaska County Conservation District, MI
- Kalkaska County Road Commission, MI
- Cheboygan County Road Commission, MI
- Presque Isle County Road Commission, MI
- Otsego County Road Commission, MI
- Becker County, MN
- City of Detroit Lakes, MN
- Ohio State University
- Iowa State University
- Trout Unlimited
- Ducks Unlimited
- Upper Manistee River Restoration Committee, MI
- Maple Island Log Homes of Michigan
- Pelican River Watershed District, MN
- Upper Black River Watershed Restoration Committee, MI
- Michigan Flyfishing Club
- Montmorency County Conservation Club, MI
- The Hungry Canyons Alliance, IA
- Conservation Resources Alliance, MI
- Huron Pines Resource Conservation and Development Area Council, Inc., MI
- Shell Noreast, MI
- FishAmerica Foundation
- Otsego Wildlife Legacy Society, MI
- Lowshaw Brothers, MI
- Earthworks, MI

Tin Shanty Bridge on the Black River, Michigan

Project Description:
Twelve organizations from federal, state and local government, local industry, and non-governmental organizations partnered and pooled their funding to restore Tin Shanty Bridge on the main branch of the Black River in Otsego County. Concern had grown by local groups because this road/stream crossing created a large source of sand and silt to the watershed, and prevented fish passage. The Upper Black River is renowned throughout Michigan as an outstanding native brook trout fishery. The high sediment loads, coupled with the lack of fish passage, made the restoration of this road/stream crossing a high priority for all involved parties.

Project Method:
The two culverts were removed and replaced with a 28 ft. steel span bridge.

Project Outcomes (Benefits):
Restoration of Tin Shanty Bridge has alleviated the restriction in the river, allowing the river to regain its natural flow rates and stream bed; it no longer blocks fish passage; and the bottomless span compensates for 50 year storm events. Brook trout spawning habitat is located both upstream and downstream of this road/stream crossing.

Tin Shanty Bridge on the Black River before (left) and after (right) renovation

Partners:
Huron Pines Resource Conservation and Development Area Council, Trout Unlimited, Shell Noreast, National Fish and Wildlife Foundation, Montmorency County Conservation Club, FishAmerica Foundation, Otsego Wildlife Legacy Society, Otsego Road Commission, USDA-Natural Resource Conservation Service, Michigan Department of Natural Resources, Michigan Department of Environmental Quality, and Upper Black River Watershed Restoration Committee, Lowshaw Brothers, and Earthworks.

For more information contact:
U.S. Fish and Wildlife Service, Alpena Fishery Resources Office, 145 Water Street, Alpena, MI 49707

Project Funding

$120,000

$0

■ FWS Fish Passage   ■ Partners

Tin Shanty bridge project partners

Western Iowa Streams Fish Passage Improvement Project, Iowa

Project Description:
Approximately 800 bridge crossings on Missouri River tributary streams in western Iowa are threatened by stream bed degradation. Local agencies are partnering to stabilize these bridges by manipulating the natural stream bed grade in the area. Grade control structures are being constructed with a 4:1 downstream slope, with a vertical elevation of 2 to 25 feet above the pre-construction stream bed. Unfortunately, the unintended consequence of stream bed grade stabilization has been a precipitous decline in native fish populations, because many of these structures are believed to be functioning as barriers to fish migration.

Project Method:
This project modified six structures on Walnut Creek, a Missouri River tributary, to a 20:1 downstream slope. Follow-up evaluation showed this action restored fish passage capabilities at these structures.

Project Outcomes (Benefits):
All modifications restored 60 miles of stream habitat for channel catfish, flathead catfish, flathead chub, Topeka shiner, paddlefish and sauger.

Streambed grade control preventing fish passage

Renovated streambed providing fish passage

Partners:
The Hungry Canyons Alliance, Iowa Department of Natural Resources, USDA Natural Resources Conservation Service, and Iowa State University.

For more information contact:
U.S. Fish and Wildlife Service, Columbia Fishery Resources Office, 608 East Cherry Street, Columbia, MO 65201

Project Funding

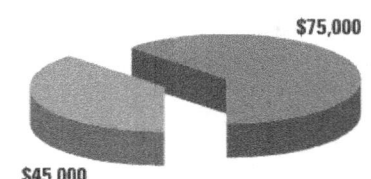

$75,000

$45,000

■ FWS Fish Passage   ■ Partners

Manistee River, Michigan

Project Description:
Located in Kalkaska County, Michigan, the Sharon Road crossing on the Manistee River impounded water during precipitation events, resulting in increased water temperature and eroded riverbanks. Due to lack of proper ditches and sediment basins, stormwater ran down the road, directly into the river, carrying its sediment.

Project Method:
The improperly designed road culvert was replaced with a single-span wooden bridge at Sharon Road on the North Branch of the Manistee River.

Bridge reconstruction on the North Branch Manistee River at Sharon Road.

Project Outcomes (Benefits):
This project provided access to 12 additional stream miles for brook trout, brown trout, and several other species, during all types of flow conditions, for spawning, rearing and feeding. Construction of the timber bridge and hardening of the road surface also alleviated the sediment runoff associated with the crossing.

Partners:
Conservation Resources Alliance, Huron Pines Resource Conservation and Development Area Council, Inc., Trout Unlimited-Paul Young Chapter, Kalkaska County Conservation District, Kalkaska County Road Commission, Michigan Department of Natural Resources, Michigan Department of Environmental Quality, Upper Manistee River Restoration Committee, USDA-Natural Resources Conservation Service, Maple Island Log Homes of Michigan, and USFWS-Partners for Fish and Wildlife Program.

For more information contact:
U.S. Fish and Wildlife Service, Alpena Fishery Resources, Office, 145 Water Street, Alpena, MI 49707

Project Funding

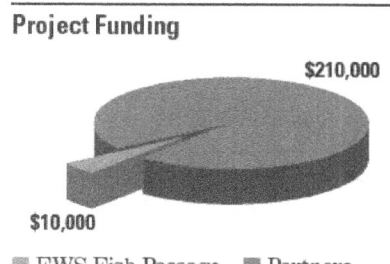

$210,000

$10,000

▨ FWS Fish Passage   ▨ Partners

Graveyard Creek, Wisconsin

Project Description:

Historically, logging has altered the Graveyard Creek watershed by replacing old growth conifers and hardwoods with shorter-lived aspen, increasing the beaver population. Because of beaver dams and log jams, Graveyard Creek had become seriously braided, causing sediment to cover spawning substrate throughout a section of the stream. The Bad River Tribe has removed beaver dams to restore Graveyard Creek to one channel. The Tribe has also installed wing dams and other in-stream modifications to create pools and began planting native trees to replace those removed during the logging era. The Tribe will continue to manage the watershed to restore coniferous and hardwood forests, which is expected to reduce or prevent reoccurring beaver populations and stream habitat problems.

Project Method:

A five mile section of habitat has been affected by beaver dam activity. Once a single channel has been established, these 5 miles will be restored to riverine habitat conditions.

Project Outcomes (Benefits):

Increased water flow will scour the sediment and expose the spawning substrate for coaster brook trout. The new wing dams and pools created by this project will benefit juvenile coasters by providing resting, feeding, and overwintering habitat.

Partners:

Bad River Tribe and USFWS Coastal Program.

For more information contact:

U.S. Fish and Wildlife Service, Ashland Fishery Resources Office, 2800 Lake Shore Drive East, Ashland, WI 54806

Beaver dam removal project on Graveyard Creek.

Dutton Locks on the Pelican River (Red River Basin), Minnesota

Project Description:
Fish passage in the Red River Drainage is a high priority for fishery managers working within this watershed. The Pelican River is a tributary to the Ottertail River that flows into the Red River. The Dutton Locks dam on the Pelican River, near Detroit Lakes, Minnesota, restricted fish movement in the river and in the Red River drainage. Lake sturgeon have been recently stocked into the Ottertail River and Detroit Lake as part of a recovery effort.

Project Method:
The existing dam located at the Dutton Locks was removed and replaced with a single channel rock rapids with step pools and a ford crossing, providing access to 10 miles of riverine habitat in the Pelican River.

Project Outcomes (Benefits):
Lake sturgeon now have access to additional habitat, thereby increasing the chances of success for lake sturgeon recovery. Restoring these connections, and allowing fish passage, increased habitat availability for all fish.

Partners:
Minnesota Department of Natural Resources, City of Detroit Lakes, Becker County, and the Pelican River Watershed District.

For more information contact:
U.S. Fish and Wildlife Service, LaCrosse Fishery Resources Office, 555 Lester Ave., Onalaska, WI 54650

Removal of the Dutton Locks and installation of step pools on the Pelican River (MN DNR photo).

Project Funding

$157,000

$20,000

■ FWS Fish Passage ■ Partners

Region 4 – Southeast

Tom Sinclair – Fish Passage Program Coordinator
U.S. Fish and Wildlife Service
1875 Century Boulevard Suite 250
Atlanta, Georgia 30345

The southeastern U.S. is home to over 60% of all the fish species within North America north of Mexico. These species support recreational and commercial fisheries valued at hundreds of millions of dollars. Dams, channelization, dredging, mining, and exotic species have all contributed to physically degraded habitats, decreased or eliminated water flows, and fragmented and displaced native populations.

Since 1999, the Southeast Region and its partners have initiated 17 projects to improve fish passage in a variety of ways. These projects directly improved passage to over 800 miles of riverine habitat by identifying barriers, planning watershed passage needs, removing artificial barriers, identifying alternative operating procedures for locks and dams, and monitoring ecosystem responses. An additional 1,500 miles were indirectly improved by these projects.

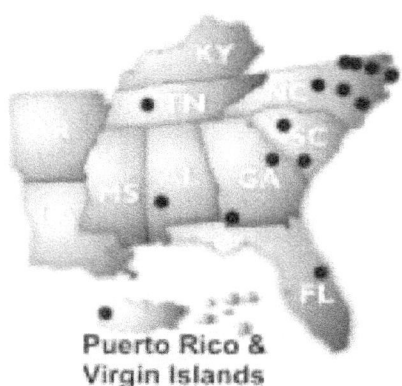

Location of Fish Passage Program projects in Region 4, 1999-2001.

National Fish Passage Program projects in USFWS Region 4, 1999-2001

State	Project Title	Project Type	Year Funded
AL	Claiborne Lock and Dam*	Assessment	1999
NC	Rains Mill Dam – Neuse River Basin*	Dam Removal	1999
FL	Merritt Island NWR*	Dike Removal	1999
SC/NC	Santee-Cooper Basin Diadromous Fish Passage Restoration Plan	Restoration Plan	1999
NC	North Carolina GIS Database	Barrier Inventory	1999
NC	Quaker Neck Dam Removal Evaluation*	Dam Removal Evaluation	1999
NC	Delineation of Historic Diadromous Fish Distribution and Abundance	Study	1999
NC/VA	Restoring Access to Roanoke River	Fishway Design	1999
FL	Merritt Island NWR*	Flow Improvement	2000
FL/GA	Woodruff Lock and Dam Evaluation	Study	2000
NC	Lake Mattamuskeet Passage	Water Control Improvement	2000
TN	Tennessee River Dam Inventory	Barrier Inventory	2000
SC/GA	New Savannah Bluff Lock and Dam	Fishway Design	2001
P.R.	Coloso Dam on the Culebrinas River*	Fishway Design	2000-2001
SC	Granby Dam Removals	Dam Removal Study	2001
NC	Chowan River	Culvert Renovation	2001

* Highlighted on the following pages.

These partners contributed funds and cooperative efforts toward accomplishments in restoring fish passage in Region 4. Their contributions are gratefully acknowledged.

- U.S. Army Corps of Engineers
- U.S. Marine Corps
- U.S. Geological Survey – Conte Anadromous Fish Laboratory
- USFWS – Coastal Program.
- National Marine Fisheries Service
- Alabama Department of Conservation and Natural Resources
- Geological Survey of Alabama
- North Carolina Division of Water Resources
- North Carolina Wildlife Resources Commission
- North Carolina Marine Fish Commission
- North Carolina Division of Marine Fisheries
- North Carolina Department of Transportation
- North Carolina Division of Emergency Management
- South Carolina Department of Natural Resources
- South Carolina Electric and Gas
- Puerto Rico Infrastructure Improvement Agency
- Puerto Rico Aqueducts and Sewers Authority
- Puerto Rico Water Company
- Puerto Rico Department of Natural and Environmental Resources
- Georgia Department of Natural Resources
- Tennessee Division of Water Supply
- Volusia County Mosquito Control District, FL
- East Carolina University, NC
- Cornell University, NY
- National Wildlife Federation
- Northwest Florida Aquatic Preserves – Dept. of Environmental Protection
- St. John's River Water Management District, FL
- Carolina Power and Light Company, NC

Claiborne Lock and Dam, Alabama

Project Description:
This project was an evaluation of fish movements and habitat use above, below, and through the Claiborne Lock and Dam on the Alabama River in the Mobile River Basin. By tracking tagged fish, the Geological Survey of Alabama was able to document river discharge levels needed for fish passage over the structure, determine the extent of spawning migrations (300+ miles in some instances), and identify an extreme fidelity for specific habitat zones.

Project Method:
The information collected was an important first step towards designing a fishway to enhance fish passage.

Project Outcomes (Benefits):
Fish passage capabilities will target blue sucker, river redhorse, smallmouth buffalo, and other species to access over 60 miles of mainstem spawning and rearing habitat previously accessible only during years of extremely high river discharge.

Claiborne Lock and Dam

Partners:
U.S. Army Corps of Engineers, Alabama Department of Conservation and Natural Resources, Geological Survey of Alabama, private entities.

For more information contact:
U.S. Fish and Wildlife Service, Daphne Ecological Services Office, 1208B Main Street, PO Drawer 1190, Daphne, AL 36526

Project Funding

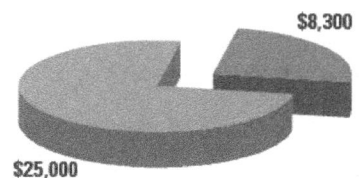

$8,300

$25,000

■ FWS Fish Passage   ■ Partners

Rains Mill Dam Removal – Neuse River Basin, North Carolina

Project Description and Method:
This project removed Rains Mill Dam on the Little River (Neuse River Basin), NC in November 1999. A partnership led by the U.S. Fish and Wildlife Service resulted in the removal of this 270-foot-long, 10-foot-high barrier. This was the third dam removal project completed as part of a larger initiative to restore fish passage at five sites in the Neuse River Basin.

Project Outcomes (Benefits):
Removal opened up 151 miles of suitable spawning and rearing habitat for alewife, blueback herring, American shad, American eel, hickory shad, striped bass, Atlantic sturgeon, and shortnose sturgeon. Elimination of the associated 28 acre impoundment will also allow reoccupation of the site by two species of endangered freshwater mussel.

Partners:
North Carolina Division of Water Resources, U.S. Army Corps of Engineers, U.S. Marine Corps, National Wildlife Federation, North Carolina Wildlife Resources Commission, and the USFWS Coastal Program.

For more information contact:
U.S. Fish and Wildlife Service, Raleigh Ecological Services Office, 551-F Pylon Drive, PO Box 33726, Raleigh, NC 27636

Stream site before dam removal (top and bottom)

Project Funding

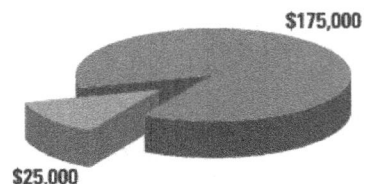

$175,000

$25,000

▨ FWS Fish Passage ▧ Partners

Stream site after dam removal

Dike Removal at Merritt Island National Wildlife Refuge, Florida

2 Projects

Project Description and Method:
The Merritt Island National Wildlife Refuge lies within the Mosquito Lagoon-Indian River-Banana River estuary complex of east-central Florida. Over 40 years ago, important high marsh habitats were completely cut off by a one mile dike that was built during construction of the Kennedy Space Center. This impoundment had been previously breached for tidal access at the north and south ends, however, true hydrological restoration was not achieved due to the remaining structure. This dike was removed in 1999; however, elevations of fill remained in the estuary that restricted outflows of rainwater and impeded passage of some fish. Other funds were used to grade the fill to an elevation that allowed free flowing water and fish passage.

Project Outcomes (Benefits):
Removal of the 1 mile dike, followed by flow improvements, provided unrestricted tidal flows and fish passage into 38 acres of former salt marsh at the Merritt Island National Wildlife Refuge. Red drum, snook, tarpon, black drum, spot, and striped mullet can now pass between the marsh and ocean habitats.

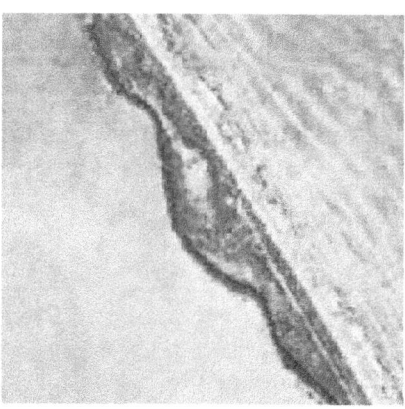

1996 aerial photograph showing dike (black line) before being removed

Turbidity barrier crossing the south breach of the impoundment

Partners:
Volusia County Mosquito Control District and the St. John's River Water Management District.

For more information contact:
U.S. Fish and Wildlife Service, Merritt Island NWR, State Road 402, P.O. Box 6504, Titusville, FL 32782

Project Funding

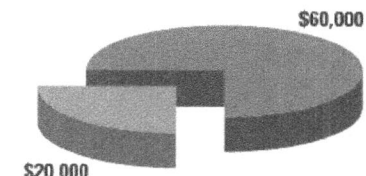

$60,000

$20,000

■ FWS Fish Passage   ■ Partners

Quaker Neck Dam Removal Evaluation, North Carolina

Project Description and Methods:
This project performed an evaluation of American shad and striped bass movement and habitat use above the recently removed Quaker Neck Dam on the Neuse River. Removal of Quaker Neck dam was one of five dams removed as part of a larger initiative to restore fish passage in the Neuse River Basin.

Project Outcomes (Benefits):
The evaluation found that both American shad and striped bass were spawning upstream of the former dam site. Complete access was provided to 79 miles of suitable spawning and rearing habitat by removal of the Quaker Neck dam.

Partners:
North Carolina Marine Fish Commission, North Carolina Wildlife Resources Commission, U.S. Geological Survey, and Carolina Power and Light Company

For more information contact:
U.S. Fish and Wildlife Service, Raleigh Ecological Services Office, 551-F Pylon Drive, PO Box 33726, Raleigh, NC 27636

Stream site during dam removal   *Stream site after dam removal*

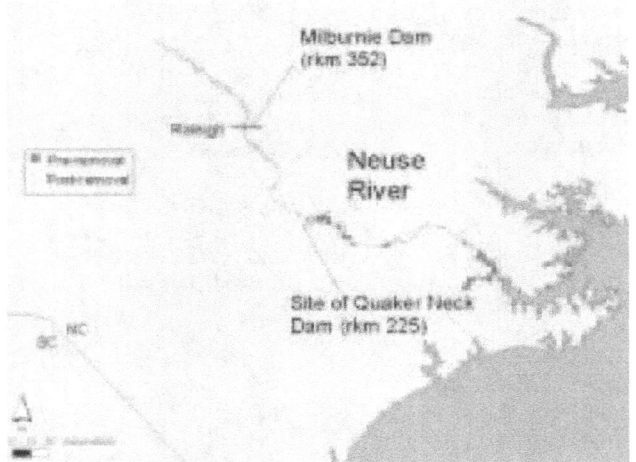

Striped bass spawning locations before and after dam removal

Project Funding

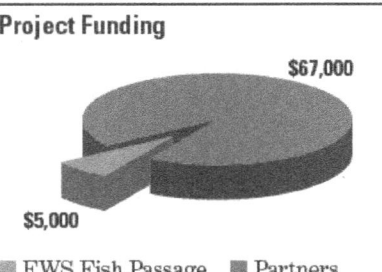

$67,000

$5,000

▨ FWS Fish Passage   ▦ Partners

Coloso Dam on the Culebrinas River, Puerto Rico

Project Description and Methods:
Since the 1930s, the Coloso Dam on the Culebrinas River has impeded or blocked access to river habitat. A fishway has been designed for this 10 foot high barrier, located 1.5 miles upstream from the mouth of the Culebrinas River. Project partners in Puerto Rico will refine the design and implement construction the fishway.

Project Outcomes (Benefits):
Construction of a fishway will open access to 130 miles of river habitat for American eel, river goby, Sirajo goby, mountain mullet, and thirteen species of migratory shrimp.

Partners:
Puerto Rico Infrastructure Improvement Agency, Puerto Rico Water Company, Puerto Rico Department of Natural and Environmental Resources, Puerto Rico Aqueducts and Sewers Authority, and the USGS-Conte Fish Laboratory.

For more information contact:
U.S. Fish and Wildlife Service, Boqueron Ecological Services Office, Carr. 301, KM5.1, PO Box 491, Boqueron, Puerto Rico 00622

Coloso Dam on the Culebrinas River

Shrimp attempting to migrate over the Coloso Dam

Project Funding

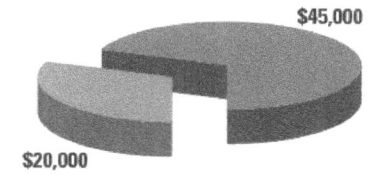

$45,000

$20,000

▨ FWS Fish Passage   ▨ Partners

Region 5 – Northeast

Dan Kuzmeskus – Fish Passage
Program Coordinator
U.S. Fish and Wildlife Service
300 Westgate Center Drive
Hadley, MA 01035

Chris Castiglione – Assistant
Program Coordinator
U.S. Fish and Wildlife Service
405 North French Road Suite 120A
Amherst, NY 14228

The Northeast Region works with states and other partners to restore and protect a variety of fish species, including Atlantic salmon, striped bass, American shad, weakfish, winter flounder, Atlantic sturgeon, and lake trout. Stable fish populations indicate healthy river systems that can provide ample fishing and recreational opportunities.

Since 1999, the Fish Passage Program in Region 5 has initiated 7 projects that improved fish passage by removing dams and designing and building fishways. These projects have directly improved passage to 502 miles of riverine habitat and over 1,000 acres of wetland area. In addition, Region 5 has been successful in establishing partnerships with Federal and State agencies to identify fish passage barriers within State or watershed boundaries. This work is part of a larger Fish Passage Program initiative to develop a Fish Passage Decision Support System. The Decision Support System will be geographically referenced, with barrier location, associated species and habitat information. In early 2003, the database will be available on the internet to identify fish barriers and aid in planning solutions.

National Fish Passage Program projects in USFWS Region 5, 1999-2001

State	Project Title	Project Type	Year Funded
ME	Pleasant Lake*	Fish Ladder	1999
ME	East Machias River*	Dam Removal	2000
PA	Manatawney Creek	Dam Removal	2000
PA	Good Hope Dam*	Dam Removal	2001
NH	Wiswall Dam on the Lamprey River	Fish Ladder or Dam Removal	
MA	Middlesex Dam on the Concord River	Breach Stabilization	2001
VA	Appomattox River (Abutment Dam)	Fishway	2001

* Highlighted on the following pages.

Location of Fish Passage Program projects in Region 5, 1999-2001

These partners contributed funds and cooperative efforts toward accomplishments in restoring fish passage in Region 5. Their contributions are gratefully acknowledged.

- National Park Service
- USDA Natural Resource Conservation Service
- U.S. Environmental Protection Agency
- U.S. Army Corps of Engineers
- U.S. Geological Survey
- U.S. Air Force
- National Marine Fisheries Commission
- National Fish and Wildlife Foundation
- Maine Department of Marine Resources
- Maine Department of Inland Fisheries and Wildlife
- Maine Department of Transportation
- Virginia Department of Game and Inland Fish
- Massachusetts Department of Fish and Wildlife
- Massachusetts Department of Marine Fisheries
- New Hampshire Department of Fish and Game
- New Hampshire Department of Environmental Services
- Pennsylvania Department of Environmental Protection
- City of Petersburg, VA
- Town of East Machias, ME
- Town of Stetson, ME
- Town of Durham, NH
- University of New Hampshire Facilities Services
- Lamprey River Advisory Committee, NH
- Dufresne-Henry Inc., NH
- FishAmerica Foundation
- Trout Unlimited
- American Rivers
- Coastal Conservation Association
- Hackle and Tackle Club, NH
- Upper Pottstown Watershed Association, PA
- Charles George Landfill Remediation, MA
- Maine Atlantic Salmon Commission
- Atlantic Salmon Federation
- Downeast Salmon Federation, ME

Pleasant Lake, Maine

Project Description:

In 1998, the Edwards Dam on the Kennebec River was removed, permitting anadromous fish to migrate an additional 17 miles upstream to the confluence of the Sebasticook River. Fish migrations in the Sebasticook River are blocked by three hydropower dams and four non-hydropower dams, including Pleasant Pond Dam. Installing a fish ladder at Pleasant Pond Dam is part of a larger initiative to restore fish passage at these seven sites in the Sebasticook River Basin. For example, fish passage projects are currently pending for implementation at the three other non-hydro dams in spring and summer, 2002.

Project Methods:

A Denil steeppass fishway was installed, allowing alewives upstream migration to spawning habitat. Providing fish passage at Pleasant Pond Dam was a key step in completing a large-scale restoration effort in the Sebasticook River Basin.

Pleasant Pond dam before fish passage was provided

Fish ladder installed at Pleasant Pond dam

Project Outcomes (Benefits):

The fishway provided access to spawning habitat for an estimated 26,880 adult alewife annually. Passage was provided to the 768-acre Pleasant Pond. Providing passage at all four non-hydropower dams will result in the restoration of 28 river miles of habitat for anadromous fish. This restoration effort will also restore habitat for Atlantic salmon, blueback herring, striped bass, and American eel.

Partners:

USFWS Coastal Program and Maine Anadromous Fish Program, Natural Resources Conservation Service, Maine Department of Marine Resources, American Rivers, Town of Stetson

For more information contact:

U.S. Fish and Wildlife Service, Gulf of Maine Program, 4R Fundy Road, Falmouth, ME 04105

Project Funding

$70,000

$20,000

■ FWS Fish Passage   ■ Partners

East Machias River, Maine

Project Description:

The East Machias Dam, located near head-of-tide on one of Maine's eight "wild" salmon rivers, was constructed in 1926 to produce power. The dam has not produced power since the late 1950's, and in the late 1960's, the Town of East Machias purchased the dam and associated lands. The dam was breached in 1973 but remained a community eyesore and safety hazard for local residents. In addition, the dam was only passable by fish at high water. The waters immediately downstream of the dam served as a holding pen for adult Atlantic salmon and other searun fish waiting to move upstream, providing harbor seals and cormorants with easy feeding opportunities. Moreover, the dam required annual maintenance to clear away debris jams and maintain access for migrating fish.

Project Methods:

In the summer of 2000, dam removal provided free passage during all water levels, minimized predation by harbor seals and cormorants, and eliminated the need for annual maintenance.

Project Outcomes (Benefits):

Searun fish, including Atlantic salmon, alewives, shad, blueback herring and rainbow smelt, were provided access to 296 river miles from the removal of East Machias Dam.

East Machias dam before removal (see road bridge behind dam)

East Machias dam after removal

Partners:

U.S. Air Force, Natural Resources Conservation Service, USFWS Coastal Program, Maine Anadromous Fish Program and Maine Field Office, U.S. Army Corps of Engineers, Maine Atlantic Salmon Commission, Maine Department of Marine Resources, Maine Department of Transportation, Town of East Machias, Trout Unlimited, Atlantic Salmon Federation, Downeast Salmon Federation

For more information contact:

U.S. Fish and Wildlife Service, Gulf of Maine Program, 4R Fundy Rd., Falmouth, ME 04105

Project Funding

$280,000

$20,000

■ FWS Fish Passage   ■ Partners

Good Hope Dam, Pennsylvania

Project Description:
Good Hope Dam stood 6 feet high and 300 feet in length. The dam and impoundment no longer served a functional purpose, was in an advanced state of disrepair, and had no identifiable owner. It was the first blockage to migratory fishes entering Conodoguinet Creek. Removing the dam was a high profile project, with numerous partners and objectives. In addition to removal, the project includes a comprehensive riparian restoration component and monitoring of chemical, physical, and biological conditions, pre- and post-dam removal.

Project Methods:
The dam was removed in November 2001, opening 22 miles of riverine habitat. Considerable habitat improvement work has also been conducted by the Conodoguinet Creek Watershed Association.

Project Outcomes (Benefits):
Additional spawning and rearing habitat has been provided for shad, herring, alewife, and other resident fish species. The project also restored a significant reach of free flowing river and laid the groundwork for returning its ecological function, while eliminating a serious public safety hazard.

Partners:
Pennsylvania Department of Environmental Protection, American Rivers, U.S. Environmental Protection Agency, Pennsylvania Fish and Boat Commission, Pennsylvania Department of Conservation and Natural Resources, Chesapeake Bay Program, U.S. Army Corps of Engineers, National Marine Fisheries Service, U.S. Geological Survey, County Conservation District, FishAmerica Foundation, and the Conodoguinet Creek Watershed Association.

Good Hope dam before removal

Dam removal

Good Hope dam after removal

For more information contact:
U.S. Fish and Wildlife Service, Susquehanna River Coordinator, 1721 North Front Street Suite 105, Harrisburg, PA 171102

Project Funding
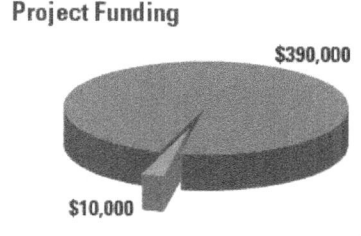
$390,000

$10,000

■ FWS Fish Passage   ■ Partners

Region 6 – Mountain-Prairie

Morgan Elmer – Fish Passage
Program Coordinator
U.S. Fish and Wildlife Service
134 Union Boulevard
Lakewood, CO 80228

The Fish and Wildlife Management
Assistance Offices throughout the
Mountain-Prairie Region support
tribal fisheries and wildlife
management programs, endangered
species recovery, control of invasive
aquatic species, and fish passage for
native species, such as cutthroat
trout, bull trout, and pallid sturgeon.

Since 1999, the Fish Passage
Program in Region 6 has initiated 8
projects that improved fish passage,
primarily at irrigation diversion
sites. These projects have directly
improved passage to 877 miles of
riverine habitat.

In 2002, new cost-share funding
opportunities are available through
the U.S. Fish and Wildlife Service
for voluntary fish screening and
passage projects associated with
water diversions in western
Montana. Fish screens placed at
entrances to water diversions can
prevent juvenile fish from swimming
into irrigation canals, thereby
decreasing mortality for these and
other native fishes.

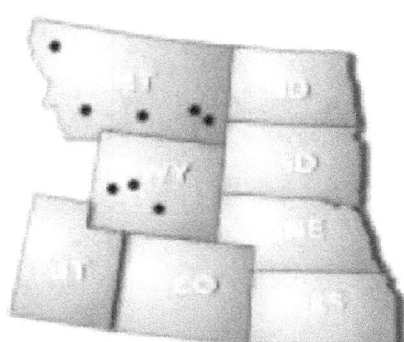

*Location of Fish Passage Program
projects in Region 6, 1999-2001*

National Fish Passage Program projects in USFWS Region 6, 1999-2001

State	Project Title	Project Type	Year Funded
MT	Soap Creek	Irrigation Diversion Improvement	1999
MT	Big Hole River	Irrigation Diversion Improvement	1999
MT	Elk Springs Creek	Culvert Renovation	2000
WY	Battle Creek	Irrigation Diversion Improvement	2001
MT	Upper Columbia River Basin Survey	Survey	2001
MT	Yellowstone River (Huntley Project)*	Irrigation Diversion Improvement	2001
WY	Mill Creek – Norwood*	Irrigation Diversion Improvement	2001
WY	Mill Creek – Chavis Drop (#1 and #2)	Grade Control	2001

* Highlighted on the following pages.

These partners contributed funds
and cooperative efforts toward
accomplishments in restoring fish
passage in Region 6. Their
contributions are gratefully
acknowledged.

- U.S. Bureau of Reclamation
- USDA Natural Resources
  Conservation Service
- U.S. Bureau of Indian Affairs
- USFWS – Partners for Fish and
  Wildlife Program
- Crow Indian Nation Fish and
  Wildlife Department, MT
- Shoshone Tribe of the Wind River
  Reservation, WY
- Arapahoe Tribe of the Wind River
  Reservation, WY
- Montana Department of Fish,
  Wildlife and Parks
- Wyoming Game and Fish
  Department
- Arctic Grayling Recovery
  Program, MT
- Snake River Conservation
  District, MT

Yellowstone River (Huntley Project), Montana

Project Description:
Huntley Diversion Dam is a concrete irrigation structure on the Yellowstone River, downstream from Billings, MT. It is over 9 feet high and creates a complete barrier to upstream fish movement except during high flows, when a bypass channel flows around the dam. The dam suffered structural damage after the last flood on the Yellowstone and required major repairs. As part of the permitting process to reconstruct the dam, enhanced fish passage was included in the project.

Project Methods:
The passage, which provides access to over 100 miles of river habitat, is a roughened channel around the north end of the dam. It has large exposed boulders strategically placed to create the proper gradient and an attractive flow to guide fish from the downstream end, up through 13 drops of the fishway, to above the diversion dam.

Project Outcomes (Benefits):
Native species benefitted include shovelnose sturgeon, pallid sturgeon, paddlefish, sauger and native cyprinids.

Huntley irrigation diversion dam on the Yellowstone River

Fish passage channel around the Huntley dam

Partners:
Montana Department of Fish, Wildlife and Parks and U.S. Bureau of Reclamation.

For more information contact:
U.S. Fish and Wildlife Service, Montana Fish and Wildlife Management Assistance Office, 4052 Bridger Canyon Road, Bozeman, MT 59715

Fish passage channel, looking downstream

Mill Creek, Wyoming

Project Description:
In the spring of 2000, an aerial survey was conducted on Mill Creek. Nine fish passage barriers were identified within a 20 mile reach of stream, including three diversion structures and six drop structures. All of the structures spanned the entire width of the stream.

Project Methods:
Two drop structures and one major irrigation diversion (shown here) were replaced with natural rock structures.

Project Outcomes (Benefits):
This project opened 15 stream miles and 25 acres of historic spawning and rearing habitat for native cutthroat trout, sauger, burbot and mountain whitefish and non-native brown trout. A by-product is a more natural looking stream with enhanced aesthetic qualities.

Partners:
USDA-National Resource Conservation Service, U.S. Bureau of Indian Affairs, and the Shosone and Arapahoe Tribes of the Wind River Reservation.

For more information contact:
U.S. Fish and Wildlife Service, Lander Fish and Wildlife Management Assistance Office, 170 North First Street, Lander, WY 82520

Norwood structure on Mill Creek, before (left) and after (right) renovation

Project Funding

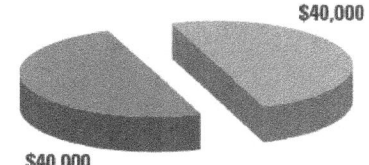

$40,000

$40,000

▨ FWS Fish Passage   ▨ Partners

Region 7 – Alaska

Michael Roy – Fish Passage
Program Coordinator
U.S. Fish and Wildlife Service
1011 East Tudor Road
Anchorage, AK 99503

Salmon are fundamental to Alaska's economy, and its social and ecological vitality. Salmon produced in Alaskan rivers support recreational and commercial fisheries valued at hundreds of millions of dollars annually, and are central to subsistence lifestyles. Salmon also play keystone ecological roles by transporting nutrients from marine to freshwater ecosystems, contributing to the productivity of rivers, lakes, wetland, and forests.

Habitat loss, overexploitation, and introduction of non-native species pose well-known threats to Alaska's salmon populations. Lesser-known, but equally important threats to healthy salmon runs are artificial barriers that block fish from essential freshwater habitats.

Recent surveys have demonstrated that thousands of culverts, underlying major highways, city streets and forest trails, block fish. Multiple barriers on a single watershed contribute to decreased escapements and reductions in angling and subsistence opportunities. The Fish Passage Program is an important cooperative effort to correct fish passage problems.

Since 1999, the Fish Passage Program and its partners have removed 15 barriers to anadromous fish, opening more than 200 stream miles to salmon, trout, grayling and other species. Most projects have replaced poorly designed or undersized culverts with larger structures that allow movement of both adult and juvenile fish.

These partners contributed funds and cooperative efforts toward accomplishments in restoring fish passage in Region 7. Their contributions are gratefully acknowledged.

- U.S. Army Corps of Engineers
- National Marine Fisheries Service
- Bureau of Land Management
- USFWS – Partners for Fish and Wildlife and Coastal Programs
- Alaska Department of Fish and Game
- Alaska Department of Natural Resources
- Alaska Department of Transportation
- Fairbanks Soil and Water Conservation District
- City of North Pole
- Matanuska-Susitna Borough
- Fairbanks North Star Borough
- Airway Road Service District
- University of Alaska, Fairbanks
- Yukon River Drainage Fisheries Association
- Chena-Badger Slough Citizen's Advisory Group,
- Dillingham Middle School
- Meadow Lakes School
- Trout Unlimited
- Williams Petroleum
- Alyeska Pipeline Service Company
- Sandstrom and Sons, Inc.
- Koncor Forest Products

National Fish Passage Program projects in USFWS Region 7 (Alaska), 1999-2001

Project Title	Project Type	Year Funded
Matanuska-Susitna Valley Culvert Survey*	Barrier Inventory	2000
Bodenburg Creek	Culvert Renovation	2000
Kenai Peninsula Culvert Survey	Barrier Inventory	2000
Chester Creek	Fish Ladder and Culvert	2000
Squaw Creek*	Culvert Renovation	2001
Orchid Lake	Culvert Renovation	2001
Duck Creek	Culvert Renovation	2001
Miller Creek	Culvert Renovation	2001
Beaver Creek	Culvert Renovation	2001
Two Moose Creek	Culvert Renovation	2001
Cottonwood Creek	Culvert Renovation	2001
Crooked Lake	Culvert Renovation	2001
Cloudy Lake	Culvert Renovation	2001
Chatanika River*	Dam Removal	2001
Chena-Badger Slough*	Culvert Renovation	2001

* Highlighted on the following pages.

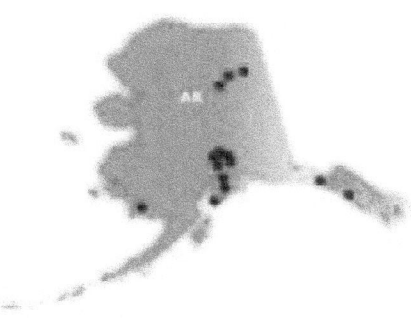

Locations of Fish Passage Program projects in Region 7, 1999-2001

Matanuska-Susitna Valley Culvert Survey, Alaska

Project Description and Methods:
The Matanuska-Susitna Valley is one of Alaska's fastest growing residential areas. The USFWS and the Alaska Department of Fish and Game inventoried 173 structures on secondary roads in several area watersheds. Final analysis is still underway, but initial reviews suggest that close to 90% of the culverts do not allow passage of anadromous fish at some life stage.

Project Outcomes (Benefits):
Data from this survey will be incorporated into the USFWS Fish Passage Decision Support System (see Introduction Section), which will allow resource managers to plan and prioritize fish passage problems. Results of the survey have led to greatly increased interest in fish passage restoration by the Matanuska-Susitna Borough (County) government.

For more information contact:
U.S. Fish and Wildlife Service, Regional Fish Passage Coord., 1101 East Tudor Road, Anchorage, AK 99503

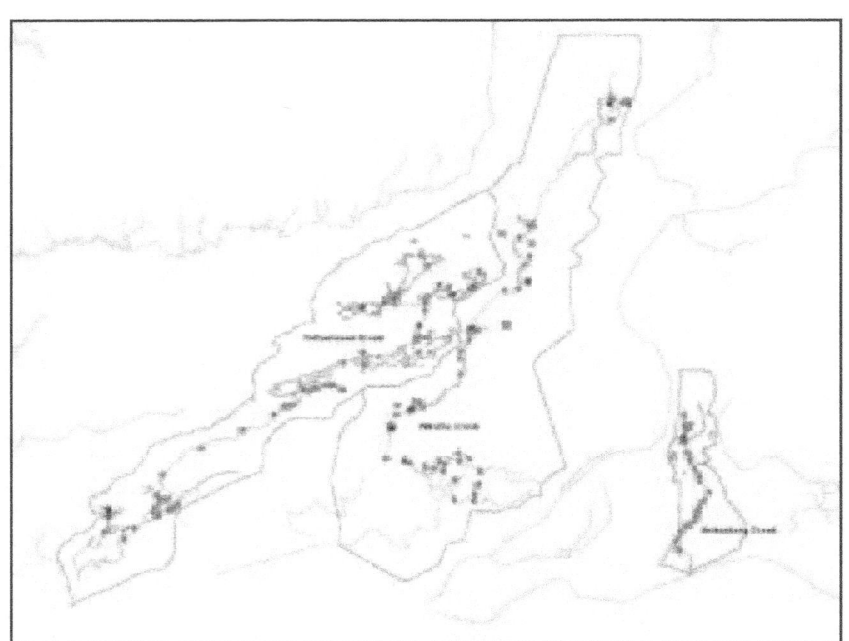

Watershed barrier inventory in the Matanuska-Susitna Valley, AK

Project Funding

$37,300

$14,500

■ FWS Fish Passage   ■ Partners

Squaw Creek, Alaska

Project Description and Method:
Culverts installed in the 1970's on Squaw Creek are undersized for the currentflow conditions and too short for present road dimensions. The poor design of the culverts eroded stream bed materials, creating a "perched" culvert that was a barrier to fish migrations during low flow periods. This project replaced two improperly installed culverts with properly designed and placed culverts, and stabilized the side slopes of the road to minimize erosion. A monitoring program, involving several partners, has also been developed to assess before and after conditions

Project Outcomes (Benefits):
After a third culvert is replaced in 2002, the project will open more than10 stream miles for adult salmon to access historical spawning grounds, for juveniles to out-migrate, and for other resident fish to use for spawning, rearing and growth.

Partners:
Alaska Department of Fish and Game, Dillingham Middle School, the City of Dillingham, and private landowners.

For more information contact:
U.S. Fish and Wildlife Service, Togiak National Wildlife Refuge, P.O. Box 270, Dillingham, AK 99576

Culvert on Squaw Creek, before (left) and after (right) renovation

Project Funding

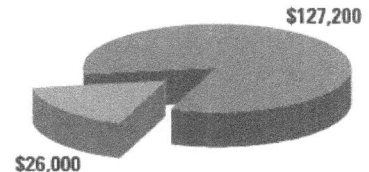

$127,200

$26,000

▨ FWS Fish Passage   ▨ Partners

Chatanika Dam, Alaska

Project Description:
In place for over 75 years, the abandoned Fairbanks Exploration Dam on the Chatanika River, a tributary of the Yukon River, blocks fish from historic spawning and rearing habitat in the upper reaches of the Chatanika River. This was the first dam removed in Alaska solely for the purpose of fisheries conservation.

Project Methods:
In January 2002, when fragile riparian areas were frozen, contractors removed the dam.

Project Outcomes (Benefits):
Chinook and chum salmon, Arctic grayling, and resident fish species were provided access to over 100 miles of historic spawning and rearing habitat.

Partners:
This project has been a cooperative venture with Alaska Department of Fish and Game, National Marine Fisheries Service, the Yukon River Drainage Fisheries Association, Bureau of Land Management, Sandstrom and Sons, Inc., and the private landowner.

For more information contact:
U.S. Fish and Wildlife Service, Fairbanks Fishery Resources Office, 101 12th Avenue, Box 17, Room 222, Fairbanks, AK 99701

Chatanika dam before removal

Removal of Chatanika dam

Project Funding

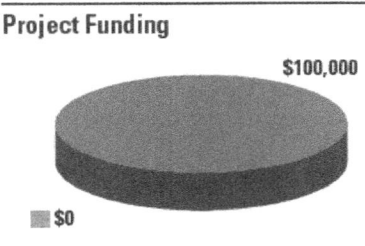
$100,000

$0

■ FWS Fish Passage   ■ Partners

After dam removal

Chena-Badger Slough, Alaska

Project Description and Methods:
This project had been identified in the recovery plan for Arctic grayling and salmon and was considered a high priority for all involved partners. Three culverts at Airway Drive of Chena-Badger Slough were removed and replaced with a single bridge.

Project Outcomes (Benefits):
The project restored passage to 5 miles of historic chinook and chum salmon and arctic grayling spawning and rearing habitat.

Partners:
USFWS-Northern Alaska Ecological Services, the City of North Pole, Fairbanks Soil and Water Conservation District, Fairbanks North Star Borough, Chena-Badger Slough Citizen's Advisory Group, Army Corps of Engineers, Alaska Department of Transportation and Public Utilities, Airway Road Service District, Alaska Department of Natural Resources, Alaska Department of Fish and Game, University of Alaska Fairbanks, Williams Alaska Petroleum, Koncor Forest Products, and Alyeska Pipeline Service Company.

For more information contact:
U.S. Fish and Wildlife Service, Fairbanks Fishery Resources Office, 101 12th Avenue, Box 17, Room 222, Fairbanks, AK 99701

Culvert at Chena-Badger Slough before (left) and after (right) renovation

Project Funding

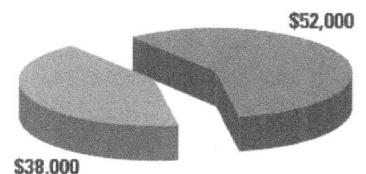

$52,000

$38,000

▨ FWS Fish Passage   ▨ Partners

Needs and Opportunities

Information for Potential Partners

The National Fish Passage Program has been effective in addressing many fish passage problems, but the existing needs far exceed these accomplishments. In 2001, the Service and its partners identified 196 fish passage projects, including 436 barriers, at an estimated cost of $44 million to complete (Fisheries Operational Needs System 2001). These are voluntary projects with willing partners and include dam removal or breaching, dike modification, installation of bypass structures such as fish ladders and screens, culvert renovation, flow modification, engineering design, and evaluation studies. Passage at these barriers would provide access to 5,983 miles and 142,830 acres of historical spawning, rearing, and feeding habitats. The Service and its partners will complete these projects as funding becomes available. It is estimated that thousands of additional barriers await identification and remedial action.

The National Fish Passage Program is looking for partners. The Program depends on good will and solid working relationships with community-minded organizations, agencies and individuals to conduct fish passage projects. Project proposals may be initiated by any individual, organization, or agency, in cooperation with the Service's Fish and Wildlife Management Assistance Offices. Project proposals must be provided to the local Fish and Wildlife Management Assistance Office by August of each year.

The following information is requested with all project proposals: title; associated management plans; partners; requested funds and matching contributions; and a project description. The project description should briefly identify the need, problem, objective, methods, and include the waterbody, location, river miles or acres opened up, and the species affected and how they will benefit.

Projects are reviewed and prioritized on a Regional basis. Funding is administered through the Fish and Wildlife Service office that is coordinating the project. The Program has flexibility from project to project, but strives to achieve a 50% funding match, including in-kind contributions.

Projects that receive the highest consideration will be those that show the greatest ecological benefits; exhibit permanence of fish passage benefits; make use of the most current scientific knowledge and proven technology; evidence the greatest public support; and generate the maximum in matching contributions.

Collaborative partnerships are also needed to expand the Fish Passage Decision Support System. Access is needed to other federal, state, or local databases that have barrier, fish, and habitat information.

For Additional Information
Contact the appropriate Regional Coordinator or your nearest Fish and Wildlife Management Assistance Office. A directory of offices is available on our web site at http://fisheries.fws.gov/fwsma/mafro.htm.

For more information on the National Fish Passage Program, visit the Program web site at: http://fisheries.fws.gov/fwsma/fishpassage.

www.ingramcontent.com/pod-product-compliance
Lightning Source LLC
Chambersburg PA
CBHW081122280526

45787CB00007B/2943